AF098809

Logged In, Burned Out: How Social Media and Menta Health Are Shaped by the Digital Age

"The internet promised connection, but somewhere along the way, we lost ourselves in the scroll. We curate, we compare, we crave validation—until we forget that who we are offline matters more than any version of us online. It's time to step back, log off, and reclaim what the algorithm can't define: our real, unfiltered selves."

Jordan R Sloane

Copyright © 2025 by Jordan R Sloane

All rights reserved.

No part of this book may be reproduced in any form or by any electronic or mechanical means, including information storage and retrieval systems, without written permission from the author, except for the use of brief quotations in a book review.

Contents

Introduction: The Digital Native Dilemma....vii

Part 1
The Self in the Age of the Internet

1. The Digital Mirror – Constructing and Curating the Self....3
2. The Algorithm Knows Me Better Than I Do....7
3. Comparison Culture & The Impostor Syndrome Epidemic....10

Part 2
Relationships in the Digital Age

4. Swiping for Connection – Love, Sex, and Dating Apps....15
5. Friendships in the Time of DMs....20
6. Family, Identity, and Digital Generational Gaps....25

Part 3
Activism, Politics, and the Power of the Online Voice

7. From Slacktivism to Real Change? The Internet and Social Movements....33
8. The Internet's Courtroom – Call-Out Culture and Digital Morality....38
9. Misinformation, Polarization, and the War on Truth....44

Conclusion: Where Do We Go From Here?....49
Epilogue: A Letter to My Younger Self About Growing Up Online....53

Introduction: The Digital Native Dilemma

I was twelve years old when I realized the internet wasn't just something I used—it was something that was using me.

It started with a simple profile picture. A grainy, low-resolution selfie taken with the family's digital camera, painstakingly uploaded to my first social media account. I remember the excitement of curating my online presence, as if the version of me that existed in pixels mattered just as much—if not more—than the one standing in front of the mirror. In that moment, I wasn't just a kid with a dial-up connection. I was a digital native, stepping into a world where identity was fluid, curated, and shaped by likes and comments.

Growing up online wasn't just about having access to the internet—it was about being shaped by it. Unlike previous generations who saw the internet as a tool, my generation experienced it as an extension of self. It wasn't just a place to gather information or send emails; it was where we formed friendships, explored our identities, fell in love, and fought for

Introduction: The Digital Native Dilemma

our beliefs. It was our playground and our battlefield, our diary and our stage.

But something felt off. The more I scrolled, the more I compared myself to people who seemed effortlessly cooler, happier, and more successful. My self-worth began to hinge on numbers: followers, likes, retweets. I crafted posts not based on what I truly felt, but on what I thought would resonate with the algorithm. My friendships were filtered through DMs and group chats, and my activism often felt like a performance rather than a passion. Was I becoming more myself online, or less? And if I stepped away from the screen, would I even recognize the person I had become?

This book is an exploration of that question. It's a deep dive into what it means to grow up in a world where our sense of self, our relationships, and even our activism are intertwined with digital culture. We'll examine how social media acts as a mirror, reflecting and distorting our identities. We'll explore the ways algorithms shape our interests and beliefs, sometimes more than we realize. We'll talk about the pressures of comparison culture, the evolving nature of digital friendships, and the blurred line between online activism and real-world impact.

And throughout, I'll share my own experiences—the highs, the lows, and the in-betweens of growing up in a space where the internet wasn't just a tool but a way of life. This isn't just my story, though. It's the story of an entire generation navigating the complexities of selfhood in an era where the digital and the real are no longer separate worlds, but two sides of the same existence.

Introduction: The Digital Native Dilemma

So, let's take a step back. Let's look at how we got here, what it's doing to us, and most importantly—where we go from here.

Part 1

The Self in the Age of the Internet

"The internet gave me a mirror, but over time, I stopped recognizing the face staring back at me. Maybe it's time to step away and remember who I was before the algorithm decided for me."

Chapter 1
The Digital Mirror – Constructing and Curating the Self

How Social Media Became an Extension of Self-Identity

I remember the first time I uploaded a profile picture. It was a grainy webcam selfie, slightly off-center, with a forced half-smile. It wasn't just an image—it was an identity marker, a digital version of myself meant to be seen, judged, and acknowledged. At the time, I didn't realize what I was stepping into. Social media wasn't just a tool for connection; it was an extension of self, a mirror reflecting not just who I was but who I wanted to be.

As platforms evolved from MySpace to Facebook, then Instagram and TikTok, our digital selves became more than static images—they became narratives. Our online presence wasn't just a snapshot but a curated story, a highlight reel carefully crafted to project the best, most digestible versions of ourselves. The internet stopped being a place we visited; it became an ever-present layer of reality, seamlessly intertwined with how we see ourselves and how we want others to see us.

The Pressure of the "Personal Brand" from Adolescence

It started subtly—a friend's vacation post with perfect lighting, a classmate's carefully composed status update, the growing number of likes becoming an unspoken measure of worth. In my early teens, social media was less about sharing and more about performing. The pressure to create a consistent, aesthetically pleasing, and engaging online presence became suffocating.

By the time I reached high school, the concept of a "personal brand" had trickled down from influencers to everyday users. It was no longer enough to just be online; you had to be strategic. What colors matched my Instagram grid? Was my Twitter persona witty enough? Did my TikTok videos align with the ever-changing trends? Every post felt like a micro-resume, a portfolio for a life that, in reality, was messier, more complex, and less curated than the one I portrayed.

Even those who weren't influencers were influenced. The idea of authenticity became paradoxical—performative in itself. We were expected to be "real," but only in ways that fit within the accepted aesthetic of vulnerability: a carefully posed crying selfie, a caption that seemed spontaneous but had been rewritten ten times. The line between genuine self-expression and strategic self-promotion blurred, leaving many of us wondering—who am I when no one is watching?

Self-Surveillance: The Rise of Filters, Selfies, and Aesthetic Perfection

I remember the first time I used a filter that altered my face. It smoothed my skin, widened my eyes, and gave me the kind of subtle glow that I had spent years chasing through skincare routines. It wasn't just a tool; it was a transformation.

Filters and editing apps quickly became more than enhancements; they were expectations. A raw, unedited selfie started to feel like an act of defiance. The culture of self-surveillance—constantly curating, modifying, and perfecting—became second nature. We weren't just taking pictures; we were creating hyperreal versions of ourselves.

With every story, every post, every subtle tweak, we adjusted our self-image both online and offline. We measured ourselves not just against others but against our own digitally enhanced reflections. The more I saw my filtered self, the more my real reflection in the mirror felt like a letdown.

Personal Reflection: My First Profile Picture vs. My Digital Self Today

That first webcam selfie, with its bad lighting and awkward tilt, wasn't perfect. But it was me. No filters, no curation, no strategic branding. I look back at it now, and while I cringe at the low resolution, I also miss the freedom it represented—the ability to exist online without the weight of digital perfection pressing down on my shoulders.

Today, my digital self is more polished, more aware. I know what angles work, how to craft a caption that maximizes engagement, how to balance "effortless" aesthetics with the reality of spending an hour choosing the right photo. But with that knowledge comes exhaustion, a quiet longing for the time when I didn't feel the need to shape my identity for the screen.

Jordan R Sloane

The internet gave me a mirror, but over time, I stopped recognizing the face staring back at me. And maybe, just maybe, it's time to step away and remember who I was before the algorithm decided for me.

Chapter 2
The Algorithm Knows Me Better Than I Do

How Recommendation Algorithms Shape Identity and Interests

At first, it felt like magic. I would search for one video on YouTube, and suddenly, a cascade of similar content would appear in my recommendations. The more I scrolled, the more the algorithm seemed to "know" me—curating content that aligned perfectly with my interests, reinforcing the music, fashion, and beliefs I already leaned towards. But over time, I started to wonder: was I choosing my interests, or was the algorithm choosing them for me?

Social media algorithms operate on a deceptively simple premise: engagement equals preference. The more time you spend on a certain type of content, the more you'll see it. But this creates a feedback loop—what starts as mild curiosity can turn into an all-encompassing obsession.

The Psychological Impact of Living in an "Echo Chamber"

When an algorithm decides what you see, your world begins to shrink. Over time, I noticed that my feeds had become less diverse. I wasn't encountering new perspectives; I was being served the same opinions, aesthetics, and narratives over and over again. The algorithm had turned my digital world into a hall of mirrors, reinforcing my existing beliefs rather than challenging them.

This wasn't just happening to me—it was happening to everyone. Echo chambers create a sense of certainty, making it easier to dismiss anything outside of our curated digital bubbles. The internet, once a place of discovery, was becoming an engine of repetition.

Identity Fragmentation: Are We Different People Online vs. Offline?

Scrolling through my Twitter feed, I felt witty and sharp. On Instagram, I was polished and aesthetic-driven. On TikTok, I let myself be a little more chaotic. The internet allowed me to experiment with different versions of myself, but at some point, I wondered: which version was the real me?

This fragmentation is the paradox of digital identity. Online, we can be whoever we want, but that freedom comes at a cost. Instead of one cohesive self, we become a collection of personas, shifting our tone, interests, and even values depending on the platform. Over time, the pressure to maintain these multiple identities becomes exhausting.

The Paradox of Digital Freedom vs. Algorithmic Control

The internet promises endless choice, yet algorithms increasingly dictate what we see, shaping our tastes, interests, and even our worldviews. We believe we are free to explore, but our exploration is subtly guided, leading us down paths determined by engagement metrics rather than genuine curiosity.

For years, I thought I was making my own choices online, but in reality, I was following a trail laid out by algorithms. The realization was unsettling: was I shaping my digital world, or was it shaping me?

As I step back and reassess my relationship with technology, I wonder—can I reclaim my digital autonomy, or am I forever bound to the invisible hand of the algorithm?

Chapter 3
Comparison Culture & The Impostor Syndrome Epidemic

Growing Up in the Shadow of Influencers and "Perfect" Lives

I was thirteen when I first discovered lifestyle influencers. Their perfectly curated Instagram grids, effortlessly cool outfits, and seemingly flawless lives made my everyday existence feel dull in comparison. They had it all: the travel, the beauty, the endless stream of admiration from strangers. What I didn't realize then was that I was comparing my behind-the-scenes reality to their carefully edited highlight reel.

Social media quickly became a stage, and everyone—including myself—was both an audience member and a performer. I found myself measuring my self-worth against likes, comments, and followers, even though I knew deep down that none of it was real. The constant exposure to seemingly perfect lives created a nagging feeling of inadequacy—was I doing enough? Was I successful enough? Was I even interesting?

The Myth of Authenticity in an Age of Curation

We tell ourselves we want authenticity online, but what does that even mean anymore? "Raw" and "real" moments are often just as curated as polished, picture-perfect posts. The influencers who preach vulnerability still edit their photos, still choose their words carefully, still present a version of themselves that is palatable and marketable.

Even I wasn't immune to this contradiction. I'd post a "candid" shot, only to have taken 30 different versions of it beforehand. I'd share personal thoughts, but only those that would resonate in a way that felt safe. Every time I tried to be authentic, I questioned whether I was actually just performing authenticity.

The Mental Health Cost: Anxiety, Depression, and Burnout from Digital Performance

Constant exposure to comparison culture wears on the mind. The anxiety of keeping up, the pressure to be relevant, the exhaustion from digital performance—it all takes a toll. I started noticing that I felt drained after scrolling, that my mood was tied to my online engagement, that I was restless when my posts didn't perform as well as I had hoped.

I wasn't alone. Studies show that excessive social media use is linked to higher rates of anxiety, depression, and low self-esteem. We weren't meant to be this aware of everyone else's lives all the time. The endless stream of curated perfection warps our perception of what's normal, making us feel like we are constantly falling short.

Personal Story: When I Realized I Was Chasing Validation Instead of Authenticity

There was a moment—one I still remember vividly—when I finally saw my own digital performance for what it was. I had spent hours editing a photo, crafting the perfect caption, and anxiously waiting for the engagement to roll in. When the likes slowed down, so did my mood. I felt empty, like I had failed some unspoken test. And then it hit me: I wasn't sharing my life; I was chasing validation.

That realization was both unsettling and freeing. It forced me to take a step back and question why I was putting so much weight on digital approval. I started limiting my time online, unfollowing accounts that made me feel inadequate, and focusing on sharing moments that felt genuine rather than just aesthetically pleasing.

The digital world still lures me in with its illusions of perfection, but I remind myself now: no one is as flawless as their online presence suggests. And more importantly, I don't have to be either.

Part 2
Relationships in the Digital Age

"We weren't meant to be this aware of everyone else's lives all the time. The constant exposure to curated perfection warps our perception of what's normal—until we feel like we're never enough."

Chapter 4
Swiping for Connection – Love, Sex, and Dating Apps

The Evolution of Romance: From AIM to Tinder

I still remember the thrill of my first online crush. It wasn't on Tinder, Hinge, or Bumble—those didn't exist yet. It was AOL Instant Messenger (AIM), where late-night conversations were punctuated by the clack of a keyboard and the ever-familiar *door opening* sound signaling their arrival. In those chats, romance wasn't about pictures or bios—it was about wit, connection, and who could craft the best away message to convey just the right amount of mystery.

Back then, meeting people online still felt like a subculture, something reserved for tech-savvy teens and the occasional long-distance hopeful. The idea of finding love—or even just a date—through the internet wasn't normalized yet. We whispered about MySpace romances, Facebook flings, and those who dared venture into OkCupid or Match.com. Fast forward a decade, and the stigma is gone. Now, swiping is the default.

Tinder, launched in 2012, turned dating into a game—literally. A quick left or right, a match, a notification that someone out there finds you attractive. The process became efficient, thrilling, and dangerously addictive. Hinge and Bumble followed, refining the formula, promising more meaningful connections, more control, more "seriousness." But at the core, the mechanics remained the same: we became profiles, our desirability distilled into a few images and a catchy bio.

In theory, dating apps offer endless possibility. In reality, they often bring something else—frustration, ghosting, and a growing sense that romance has turned into an algorithmic transaction.

The Dopamine Cycle of Matches, Ghosting, and Digital Rejection

A match. A rush of validation. A conversation begins—or, sometimes, it doesn't. You send a message, wait, check your phone too many times, only to be met with silence. *Ghosted*.

The cycle is exhausting but addictive. Dating apps are engineered like slot machines, built to keep us swiping, rewarding us intermittently so we never quite quit. Every match feels like a mini-win, a tiny dopamine hit that keeps us coming back. Even when we're not truly interested in a person, the validation of a match alone can be intoxicating.

And yet, for all the options, the effort, the conversations, there's an odd feeling of stagnation. Sometimes, it feels like we're just *collecting* matches rather than genuinely connecting. The abundance of choice breeds indecision. Why invest in one person when there's always the possibility of someone *better* just a swipe away?

Dating apps have created a paradox: the illusion of infinite romantic potential but the reality of emotional exhaustion.

Are We More Connected or Lonelier Than Ever?

At their best, dating apps offer opportunities that never existed before—connections across cities, countries, even continents. People who might never have crossed paths now have a chance to meet. But at their worst, they magnify modern dating's worst tendencies: superficiality, commitment-phobia, and emotional detachment.

I've had nights where I scrolled through Tinder, feeling both hopeful and hollow. The faces blurred together, the conversations felt repetitive, and I started to wonder—was I actually looking for connection, or was I just avoiding loneliness?

And then there's the dark side—where interactions aren't just disappointing but dehumanizing. Apps reduce people to profiles, making it easier to treat others as disposable. Ghosting, breadcrumbing, orbiting—all new words for age-old behaviors, but amplified by the ease of digital detachment. When a connection fades, it doesn't feel like losing a person—it feels like closing a tab.

So, are we more connected than ever, or have we just found new ways to be lonely together?

. . .

Personal Story: A Relationship That Existed Almost Entirely Online

There was a time when I truly believed I had fallen in love through a screen.

We met on a dating app—one of the many. Our conversations flowed effortlessly, spanning late-night texts, voice notes, and eventually, FaceTime calls that lasted until one of us fell asleep. He lived in another state, but that didn't seem to matter. In a way, the distance made it easier; the absence of real-world logistics allowed our connection to exist in a kind of digital utopia.

For months, we talked every day. We knew each other's schedules, our favorite songs, the random little details that make someone feel real. But at some point, the cracks began to show.

We never had to deal with awkward silences over dinner or the way someone's mood shifts in real time. Our "relationship" existed in curated moments—highlight reels of our personalities. Without shared physical space, there were no unfiltered experiences, no organic intimacy.

Eventually, we made plans to meet in person. The anticipation was electric. But when we finally stood face to face, something was... off. Not because either of us had lied, but because we had built something in our heads that real life couldn't replicate. The chemistry didn't translate. The conversations, so effortless over text, felt stilted in person. It was like meeting a stranger I already knew too well.

In the end, we drifted apart—not in a dramatic breakup, but in a quiet, inevitable fade. The way so many digital relationships do.

The Future of Love in the Age of Apps

Dating apps aren't going anywhere. They are part of modern romance, for better or worse. Some people find love. Others find fleeting validation. Many find frustration.

I don't think dating apps have ruined romance, but they've undeniably changed it. They've made connection more accessible but also more impersonal. They've given us more choices, but sometimes, too many choices lead to indecision rather than fulfillment.

For now, we keep swiping, searching, hoping that somewhere in the digital sea of faces, we'll find something real.

Or maybe, just maybe, we'll decide to put the phone down and take our chances in the real world.

Chapter 5
Friendships in the Time of DMs

How Digital Friendships Differ from Real-Life Bonds

Some of my closest friendships started in my phone.

It sounds strange to say out loud, but it's the reality of growing up online. I've built deep connections with people I've never met in person, shared inside jokes with friends I've only ever typed to, and confided in someone whose voice I've never actually heard outside of a voice memo.

Online friendships feel just as real as in-person ones—sometimes even more so. The ability to connect instantly, across time zones and social circles, makes digital friendships uniquely intimate. There's no waiting to see someone in person to vent or celebrate. The accessibility is constant.

But that accessibility is also where things get complicated. Digital friendships often lack the context of real-world interactions. There's no body language, no shared experiences in physical space. Everything exists in messages, memes, and voice notes. That means misunderstandings are easier, conflicts can escalate over text, and the depth of a connection can sometimes be deceiving.

There's something about seeing a friend's face light up in real life, about experiencing a moment together without screens between you. Online friendships are valid, but they exist in a different space—a space where connection is instant but sometimes fragile.

The Phenomenon of "Parasocial Relationships" with Influencers and Streamers

There's a strange kind of friendship that exists in the digital age: the one-sided kind.

I know people who talk about YouTubers as if they're old friends. Streamers who feel like daily companions. Influencers whose updates feel personal, even though they have millions of followers. It's called a *parasocial relationship*—a one-way emotional bond where we feel connected to someone who doesn't know we exist.

I've felt it myself. There was a time when I watched the same content creator every night, their voice filling the silence of my room. It was comforting, almost like having a friend keep me company. I knew their pet's name, their favorite coffee order, their inside jokes with their audience. And yet, if I ever ran into them in real life, they wouldn't recognize me.

These relationships aren't inherently bad. They can be a source of comfort, inspiration, even motivation. But they can also be deceptive. The illusion of intimacy makes it easy to forget that influencers are curating their personalities for an audience. They don't know us the way we feel like we know them.

It's a reminder that, no matter how personal digital spaces feel, they don't always reflect reality.

The Impact of Social Media on Deep vs. Surface-Level Friendships

Before social media, friendships took effort. If you wanted to stay in touch, you had to call, meet up, write letters. Now, staying connected is as easy as liking a post or sending a meme. But does that actually mean we're closer?

Social media has blurred the lines between *friends* and *acquaintances*. I know intimate details about people I haven't spoken to in years—where they vacationed last summer, what they had for brunch, the highlights of their life, carefully curated for their followers.

But knowing someone's updates isn't the same as knowing *them*. A deep friendship isn't built on occasional DMs or reacting to an Instagram story—it's built on real conversations, shared experiences, vulnerability.

Social media keeps people in our lives, but often in a passive way. We assume we're maintaining friendships because we see someone's posts, but we're not actually talking, not actually *there* for them in a meaningful way.

I've caught myself thinking, *I should reach out to them*, only to get distracted by scrolling. I've let friendships fade because social media gave me the illusion that they were still intact.

And I've had to remind myself that *liking* a post isn't the same as showing up for someone when they need you.

True connection takes more than just being on each other's timelines.

Losing Friends Over Text: Conflict and Cancellation Culture

Friendship breakups have always been painful. But there's something uniquely devastating about losing a friend through a screen.

In the digital age, friendships can end over a single message—or worse, no message at all. Ghosting isn't just a dating phenomenon; it happens in friendships too. The slow fade, the unanswered texts, the gradual realization that someone who once knew everything about you has stopped responding.

And then there's *cancellation culture*. One misstep, one disagreement, one out-of-context screenshot, and a friendship can implode in the public eye. The internet doesn't allow for nuance. It demands instant judgment, immediate sides.

I've seen friendships dissolve over subtweets, over vague posts that everyone *knows* are about someone specific. I've seen people dragged in comment sections, their mistakes dissected by people who were once their closest confidants.

In a world where everything is documented, where private messages can be screenshotted and conflicts can play out in real time for an audience, friendships feel more fragile than ever. One wrong move, one bad take, and suddenly, you're on the outside.

But the truth is, real friendships—the ones that matter—can withstand more than a bad tweet or a single disagreement. If a friendship falls apart over a text, maybe it wasn't built to last. If someone is willing to cut you off without a conversation, maybe they weren't really your friend to begin with.

Relearning Friendship in the Digital Age

I've had to remind myself what real friendship looks like. It's not just replying to a story, sending a funny TikTok, or commenting "love this" on a post. It's being there, in person or through a call, when it matters.

Social media has given us *more* friends, but it's also made friendship feel more disposable. It's easier than ever to stay connected, yet somehow, we've never been more at risk of feeling alone.

So I'm learning to log off. To call instead of text. To put my phone away when I'm with someone in person. To be present, really present, in the friendships that matter.

Because in the end, likes and comments fade. But real friendships—the ones built on trust, effort, and presence—those are worth holding on to.

Chapter 6

Family, Identity, and Digital Generational Gaps

The Generational Divide: Explaining Memes to My Parents

There's a unique kind of frustration in trying to explain a meme to someone who doesn't speak the language of the internet.

I remember showing my parents a meme that had me laughing for five straight minutes. The punchline was a mix of absurd humor and niche internet culture, layered with references to a trending joke from Twitter. When I handed my phone to my mom, she stared at it, confused. "I don't get it," she said, passing it back.

How could I even begin to explain? The humor wasn't just in the image or the words—it was in the *context*, the collective understanding that comes from being deeply immersed in digital culture.

The internet has created a generational gap that feels wider than ever. It's not just about technology use—it's about the way we communicate, the way we see the world. Older generations grew up with letters and phone calls. We grew up with emojis and TikTok slang. They ask why we spend so much time on our phones; we ask how they survived without Google.

This disconnect is more than just humorous misunderstandings over memes—it's a fundamental difference in how we navigate identity, relationships, and privacy.

How Social Media Shapes Family Dynamics (Facebook Moms vs. TikTok Teens)

Every generation has its own digital landscape. My parents' generation discovered social media through Facebook—posting family vacation albums, sharing inspirational quotes, using excessive ellipses in every status update. My generation grew up on Instagram, Snapchat, and Twitter—curating aesthetic feeds, speaking in GIFs, and developing an almost instinctive understanding of internet irony. Then came the next wave: Gen Z and TikTok, where trends evolve in a matter of hours, where humor is fast, chaotic, and often indecipherable to outsiders.

These different digital worlds create different social media behaviors. Parents use Facebook to keep up with family. Teens use Snapchat to keep conversations just *barely* out of parental sight. Millennials carefully craft Instagram stories, while Gen Z floods their Finstas with unfiltered chaos.

And when these worlds collide? It's awkward.

I've cringed when a relative commented on a post that wasn't meant for them, when my mom sent me a "hilarious" minion meme, when a family friend shared an embarrassing childhood photo that I *never* wanted resurfaced.

But beyond the humor, social media has reshaped how families communicate. Parents no longer just ask how school was—they check our Instagram stories. Grandparents no longer call to catch up—they scroll through our posts. The internet has made family interactions more *constant*, for better or worse.

Digital Footprints and the Struggle for Privacy from Family Online

Growing up, my parents warned me about *strangers* on the internet. What they didn't warn me about was *them* on the internet.

There's a strange irony in watching the same people who once worried about online privacy now overshare every detail of their lives. The same parents who lectured us about "being careful" post status updates about their personal lives, upload every photo from a family gathering, and forward chain messages with *zero* fact-checking.

Meanwhile, younger generations have become hyper-aware of digital footprints. We know that everything we post is permanent, searchable, and potentially regrettable. We use private accounts, burner profiles, disappearing messages. We curate our public selves carefully, because we've grown up knowing that the internet *never forgets*.

The biggest privacy invasion, though, isn't from corporations tracking our data—it's from our own families.

I can't count the number of times I've heard someone complain, *"My mom follows me on Instagram, so I can't post that."* Or, *"My aunt screenshots everything and sends it to the family group chat."* There's an unspoken digital divide: parents see social media as a *public space,* while younger generations see it as a series of carefully controlled, semi-private *micro-spaces.*

This constant surveillance changes how we express ourselves. It forces us to create separate identities—one version for family, another for friends, maybe even a secret account where we can finally just *be.*

The irony? The same people who taught us about privacy now make it nearly impossible to have any.

A Reflection on What It Means to Have a "Public" Personal Life

There was a time when privacy meant keeping your diary locked in a drawer. Now, privacy means carefully curating which parts of your life are visible to which audiences.

We live in an era where personal lives are *public by default.* Social media has turned everyone into a brand, a personality, a digital entity that can be seen, shared, and scrutinized.

I used to post without thinking—random thoughts, candid moments, unfiltered reflections. Then I learned the hard way that *the internet remembers.* A post that felt harmless in 2012 can resurface a decade later. A joke made in passing can be taken out of context. A single bad take can haunt you forever.

So, we curate. We delete. We archive old tweets, double-check captions, think twice before posting anything remotely controversial.

But sometimes, I wonder—what have we lost in the process?

I envy the older generations who treat social media casually, who post blurry photos without worrying about aesthetics, who don't overthink every status update. I envy the days when we weren't all so *aware* of our digital presence, when we didn't feel like we were constantly performing for an audience.

Because that's what social media has become—a performance. A balancing act between authenticity and acceptability. A never-ending negotiation between what we *want* to share and what we *should* share.

And when our own families are part of that audience, the lines between public and private blur even further.

So where do we draw the line?

Maybe the answer isn't deleting everything, but redefining our relationship with the digital world. Maybe it's about taking back control—not just of what we post, but of how much power we give social media over our identities, our friendships, our families.

Because in the end, who we are *offline* still matters more than any carefully curated version of ourselves online.

Final Thoughts on Family and the Digital Age

The internet didn't just change how we communicate—it changed how we exist within our own families.

It created new ways to stay connected but also new ways to misunderstand each other. It made privacy more complicated, made generational gaps feel wider, and turned personal moments into public ones.

But despite the awkwardness, the cringeworthy comments, the oversharing, and the digital surveillance—family remains family. Whether in person or online, they will always be there, watching, commenting, and occasionally, embarrassingly, reacting to our posts with.

Maybe the best we can do is set boundaries, laugh at the generational confusion, and remember that at the end of the day, *some things* are better kept off the internet.

Even if that means explaining, one more time, why we really don't want to be tagged in that Facebook photo from 2009.

Part 3
Activism, Politics, and the Power of the Online Voice

"Social media will always be there, waiting for you to scroll, compare, and consume. But life—the real, unfiltered, messy, beautiful life—is happening outside the screen. Don't miss it."

Chapter 7

From Slacktivism to Real Change? The Internet and Social Movements

The Rise of Hashtag Activism (#MeToo, #BLM, #ClimateStrike)

The first time I saw activism trending, it was surreal. I wasn't in a protest march or at a rally—I was in my bedroom, scrolling.

The internet has transformed activism from something that required physical presence into something that can happen with a click. Hashtags like #MeToo, #BlackLivesMatter, and #ClimateStrike weren't just phrases—they were movements, rallying cries that brought millions of people together online.

I remember watching as my entire feed flooded with personal stories during #MeToo. Women, some of whom had never spoken about their experiences before, shared their truths in raw, unfiltered posts. Survivors who had been silent for years finally had a space where they felt heard. It was both empowering and overwhelming—witnessing the sheer scale of injustice, all through a screen.

Movements that might have once been ignored by mainstream media found life on the internet. Black Lives Matter, which started as a hashtag after the killing of Trayvon Martin, grew into a global force. What began as online outrage turned into mass protests, policy debates, and cultural shifts. The same happened with #ClimateStrike—what started as a few activists sharing their frustration with government inaction became a worldwide youth-led climate movement, with people organizing strikes in cities around the world.

Social media gave activism new speed, new reach. But it also raised a question: *Was this real activism, or just a digital illusion of change?*

The Difference Between Performative Activism and Real-World Impact

The summer of 2020 was the moment everything changed. The world was in lockdown, and yet, despite the isolation, we were more connected than ever—especially in our collective anger. After the murder of George Floyd, protests erupted across the U.S. and beyond. But for every person marching in the streets, there were thousands more engaging from their screens.

Black squares filled Instagram on #BlackoutTuesday, meant as a symbol of solidarity. But soon, people started asking: *What does this actually do?*

That was the moment I realized how fine the line was between raising awareness and *just looking like you care.*

Posting a black square didn't dismantle racist systems. Tweeting about climate change didn't lower carbon emissions. Retweeting a thread about police brutality wasn't the same as fighting for policy change. But in the age of digital activism, these small acts felt like they *should* be enough.

I've seen people use activism as a social currency—performing outrage for likes, posting statements they don't fully understand, speaking on issues they've never researched. And I've been guilty of it too—posting about issues because it felt like the right thing to do, but not always following up with real action.

Real activism is messy. It requires risk, effort, and sometimes discomfort. Signing petitions, donating, protesting, having difficult conversations—those things don't always come with instant gratification or viral engagement.

So the question remains: *When does online activism become real-world action? And when is it just another form of self-promotion?*

A Personal Reflection on Participating in an Online Movement

There was a moment when I truly believed the internet could change everything.

I had spent hours sharing resources, joining discussions, reposting threads. The more I engaged, the more I felt like I was *doing* something. I saw people educating themselves, calling out injustice, organizing protests. It felt powerful.

But then, as the trending topics changed, so did people's attention. The black squares disappeared. The viral threads slowed down. The momentum faded.

It made me question my own role. Was I actually contributing to change, or was I just part of a digital cycle that repeats itself with every new crisis?

That realization forced me to rethink how I engage with activism online. I started looking for ways to turn awareness into action. I followed up on the causes I cared about *after* they stopped trending. I made an effort to support organizations consistently, not just when they were viral.

The internet is a powerful tool for activism, but it can't be the only tool. The real work—the uncomfortable, necessary, slow-moving work—happens beyond the screen.

Hashtag activism can start a movement, but what happens after the trend fades determines if it was ever real to begin with.

The Future of Activism in the Digital Age

The internet has changed activism forever. It has given people a voice, exposed injustices, and created global movements that might never have existed otherwise.

But it's also created a culture where activism is sometimes treated as an aesthetic rather than an action. Where people post the "right" things out of fear of being called out, rather than out of genuine conviction.

So, where do we go from here?

Maybe the answer isn't abandoning online activism but using it more intentionally. Sharing resources, but also supporting causes offline. Speaking out, but also listening. Raising awareness, but also taking action.

Because in the end, a viral hashtag can start a conversation. But change—the kind that actually matters—happens when we take what we've learned online and do something about it in the real world.

Chapter 8
The Internet's Courtroom – Call-Out Culture and Digital Morality

The Power and Dangers of "Cancellation"

It starts with a screenshot. A resurfaced tweet, an out-of-context video, a viral thread detailing someone's problematic past. Within hours, the internet turns into a courtroom, and the sentence is swift: canceled.

I remember the first time I witnessed an online cancellation unfold in real-time. It was someone I followed—someone I admired. At first, the criticism seemed justified; they had said something offensive, something harmful. But as the discourse escalated, it became clear that this wasn't just about holding them accountable—it was about *destroying* them.

Their followers turned against them. Their sponsors dropped them. People who had once praised them were now dissecting their every word, their every mistake. It wasn't just about what they had done—it was about making sure they could never come back from it.

Cancel culture started as a way to hold people accountable, especially those in power who had previously faced no consequences. It gave marginalized communities a voice, a way to demand justice when traditional systems failed them. The #MeToo movement was one of the most powerful examples—where public call-outs led to real-world consequences for powerful men who had long escaped accountability.

But somewhere along the way, cancellation became something else. It became *spectacle*.

The internet isn't a courtroom where people get fair trials. There's no due process, no room for growth or learning—just instant, permanent judgment. And once you're deemed guilty, there's no appeal.

The line between accountability and destruction has never been thinner.

The Fine Line Between Accountability and Digital Mob Justice

Accountability is necessary. Harmful behavior should be called out, and people should take responsibility for their actions. But when does holding someone accountable turn into something more sinister?

I've seen people get canceled for things they said *years ago*, long before they had the understanding they have now. I've seen creators apologizing for jokes they made as teenagers, terrified that their careers could end over something they no longer believe in.

There's a difference between exposing systemic harm and going on a digital witch hunt.

Accountability should give people a chance to learn, to change, to make amends. Digital mob justice, on the other hand, doesn't allow for that. It thrives on outrage, on quick judgments, on tearing someone down and moving on to the next target.

Social media has created a world where people are both judge and jury, where strangers decide whether someone deserves forgiveness or permanent exile. The problem? The internet never forgets, even when people do.

There's no redemption arc in cancel culture—only permanent guilt.

The Psychological Toll of Public Shaming

Being canceled isn't just about losing followers or sponsorships. It's about losing your *sense of self*.

I've seen influencers disappear from the internet entirely, their mental health shattered by the weight of public scrutiny. I've seen everyday people—those who went viral for the *wrong* reasons—lose jobs, relationships, and entire support systems overnight.

The human brain wasn't designed to handle mass shaming on a global scale. In the past, if you made a mistake, the consequences were limited to your immediate social circle. Now, a single mistake can be broadcast to millions of strangers who will judge you based on a tweet, a screenshot, a moment taken out of context.

The result? Anxiety. Depression. Isolation.

Studies have shown that social rejection triggers the same pain centers in the brain as physical pain. Now imagine that pain magnified by thousands, even millions, of people at once.

It's no wonder that so many people who have been canceled describe feeling suicidal. When the world decides you are irredeemable, where do you go from there?

And yet, the internet moves on. The mob finds a new target, a new scandal, a new person to dissect. But the person they left behind? They're still living in the ruins of what used to be their life.

A Personal Story: Witnessing (or Experiencing) the Effects of Being Called Out Online

I've never been canceled, but I've felt the fear of it.

I've deleted tweets, second-guessed my posts, hesitated before sharing an opinion—because I know how quickly the internet can turn.

But I have watched someone I know go through it.

They made a mistake. A genuine mistake. A thoughtless comment that, in real life, would have warranted a conversation, an apology, and a chance to do better. But online? There was no conversation. No room for apology. Just backlash, piling up faster than they could process it.

People they had never met called them *evil*. Strangers dug through their past, looking for more proof that they were a bad person. Friends distanced themselves, not wanting to be associated with someone "problematic."

They apologized. Sincerely. Repeatedly. But it didn't matter.

The damage was done.

Watching it unfold was terrifying. It made me realize how fragile online reputation is—how quickly the internet can decide you are unworthy of grace.

And the worst part? Most of the people who joined in the backlash probably forgot about it within days. But for the person at the center of it, the shame lasted much, much longer.

Can We Create a Culture of Accountability Without Cruelty?

So where do we go from here?

I don't think cancel culture is entirely bad. Some people *deserve* to be held accountable, especially those in power who continue to harm others. But the way we handle it needs to change.

We need to ask ourselves:

• *Is this about justice, or is it about punishment?*

• *Is this person genuinely harmful, or did they make a mistake?*

• *Are we giving them a chance to learn, or are we just enjoying their downfall?*

- *Would we want to be treated the way we are treating them?*

Accountability should be about growth, not just destruction. We need to create space for people to make mistakes, apologize, and *actually* change. Because if we don't, we're not really fighting for justice—we're just creating a culture of fear.

If we truly care about making the world a better place, we have to believe that people can change.

Otherwise, what's the point of calling them out in the first place?

Final Thoughts: The Cost of Internet Justice

The internet has given us power—the power to hold people accountable in ways that weren't possible before. But with that power comes responsibility.

It's easy to judge from behind a screen. It's easy to be outraged, to demand consequences, to join the mob. What's harder is having empathy, recognizing humanity, and understanding that people are more than their worst moments.

Cancel culture isn't going away. But maybe, just maybe, we can choose to wield it more carefully.

Because the internet may never forget—but we can choose to forgive.

Chapter 9
Misinformation, Polarization, and the War on Truth

Growing Up in the Era of Fake News and Deepfakes

The first time I fell for fake news, I didn't even realize it.

I was scrolling through Twitter when I saw a headline so shocking that I didn't even stop to question it—I just hit retweet. It wasn't until later, when someone fact-checked me in the replies, that I realized I had spread misinformation.

That was the moment I understood how easy it is to get caught in the web of digital deception.

Growing up in the internet age means living in a world where truth is constantly under attack. Clickbait headlines, AI-generated deepfakes, doctored screenshots—lies are more convincing than ever. And in the battle between facts and engagement, engagement always wins.

Fake news isn't new, but the internet has made it more powerful. Misinformation spreads faster than truth, not because people *want* to be misled, but because false information is often designed to provoke an emotional reaction. Outrage, fear, shock—these are the emotions that make people share before they think.

And that's exactly what bad actors count on.

We are no longer just consumers of information—we are *distributors* of it. With every like, share, and retweet, we have the power to spread truth or falsehoods. But in an age where fake news is everywhere, how do we even begin to tell the difference?

How the Internet Shapes Political Identity

The internet didn't just change how we get our news—it changed *who we are*.

Before social media, political identity was shaped by personal experiences, family discussions, and the occasional news broadcast. Now, it's shaped by algorithms, viral threads, and the communities we interact with online.

I've seen people's political views shift dramatically—not because they read a book or had a real-world experience, but because they fell down a social media rabbit hole. One video leads to another, one tweet leads to a thread, and suddenly, they've been radicalized by content designed to manipulate them.

It works both ways. Conservatives get pushed further right. Progressives get pushed further left. The internet doesn't encourage *understanding*—it encourages *tribalism*.

Politics has become a sport, and social media is the stadium. People don't just want to be informed; they want to *win*. They want their side to dominate, their arguments to go viral, their opponents to be *destroyed*.

But when politics becomes entertainment, we stop seeing the people on the other side as *people*. They become enemies, threats, villains. And once we dehumanize those who disagree with us, compromise becomes impossible.

The internet was supposed to give us more access to information. Instead, it gave us more ways to reinforce what we already believe.

Can We Ever Truly Escape Our Filter Bubbles?

When I open my phone, I don't see *the world*—I see *my world*.

My feed is filled with people who think like me, talk like me, believe what I believe. The algorithm ensures that I am comfortable, surrounded by opinions that validate my own.

It feels good. But it's also dangerous.

Filter bubbles—the invisible walls created by algorithms—trap us in ideological echo chambers. We stop being exposed to different perspectives. We start assuming that *everyone* thinks the way we do. And when we do encounter a differing opinion, it feels *wrong*, even threatening.

I've seen it happen to myself. When I see a take that challenges my worldview, my first instinct isn't to consider it—it's to dismiss it. To assume bad intent. To argue. To *win*.

The internet doesn't just divide us—it convinces us that the other side is beyond saving.

Escaping a filter bubble isn't easy. It requires *active* effort—seeking out diverse perspectives, reading sources we don't always agree with, questioning our own assumptions. It requires discomfort.

And discomfort isn't what the internet is designed for.

The Personal Responsibility of Being an Informed Digital Citizen

So, what do we do? How do we navigate a world where truth is under attack, where misinformation is everywhere, where polarization feels inevitable?

We take responsibility.

We fact-check before we share. We think before we react. We resist the urge to believe something just because it *feels* true.

We step outside our filter bubbles. We challenge ourselves to engage with perspectives we don't agree with—not to argue, but to understand.

We hold ourselves accountable for the information we spread, because every post, every retweet, every comment contributes to the larger digital ecosystem.

The internet isn't going to change on its own. If we want a world where truth matters, where nuance isn't lost, where people aren't reduced to enemies—*we* have to make it happen.

It starts with us.

Final Thoughts: Fighting for Truth in the Digital Age

We are the first generation to grow up online. We have watched the internet evolve from a place of possibility to a battleground for information, identity, and ideology.

We have seen the power of digital activism, the devastation of cancel culture, the chaos of misinformation. We have experienced the highs of connection and the lows of division.

And now, we face the hardest question of all: *What comes next?*

The internet isn't going away. But if we want it to be a place that fosters truth, progress, and understanding, we have to be *better* than the systems designed to manipulate us.

The fight for truth isn't just about fact-checking articles or calling out fake news. It's about changing the way we engage with information, the way we see those who disagree with us, the way we use our voices.

Because the future of the internet isn't just in the hands of tech companies, politicians, or media corporations.

It's in *ours*.

Conclusion: Where Do We Go From Here?

A Reflection on My Evolving Relationship with the Internet

I used to think of the internet as a tool—something separate from real life, a space I could enter and leave at will. But as I grew up, I realized that it wasn't just a place I visited—it was a place that shaped me.

My friendships, my self-image, my understanding of the world—all of it was influenced by the digital spaces I inhabited. I learned how to express myself online before I fully knew who I was offline. I curated, I performed, I engaged in conversations that made me feel seen and in arguments that left me exhausted.

There were times when the internet felt like an escape, a lifeline, a revolution. And there were times when it felt like a trap, an echo chamber, a battleground.

Looking back, I can see the full picture now. The internet gave me connection, but it also fueled my loneliness. It gave me information, but it also buried me in misinformation. It gave me a voice, but it also made me afraid of saying the wrong thing.

Now, as I stand at the intersection of digital culture and real life, I find myself asking: *Who am I outside of the internet?*

And more importantly: *Can I reclaim my identity from it?*

Can We Reclaim Our Identities from Digital Culture?

The internet thrives on our participation. Every click, every post, every moment of engagement adds to its power. But the more we exist online, the more we risk losing the parts of ourselves that aren't meant for an audience.

So how do we take back control?

We start by redefining our relationship with digital spaces. We remind ourselves that we are more than our social media presence, more than our curated feeds, more than the way we are perceived through a screen.

We resist the pressure to perform and embrace the freedom to simply *be*.

We let go of the idea that every moment needs to be documented, that every thought needs to be shared, that our worth is tied to engagement metrics.

We recognize that real identity isn't found in a profile—it's found in the moments that exist beyond the screen.

The Balance Between Online and Offline Life

I won't pretend that the answer is abandoning the internet entirely. That's not realistic, and frankly, it's not necessary. The digital world is a part of our reality now. But it doesn't have to consume us.

We can choose to be intentional.

We can set boundaries—taking breaks when needed, protecting our privacy, prioritizing face-to-face interactions. We can engage with the internet on *our* terms, rather than letting it dictate our self-worth.

We can remind ourselves that some of the most meaningful moments in life happen when no one is watching, when there's no post to make, no audience to perform for—just real people, real conversations, real experiences.

The internet will always be there. But life is happening outside of it, too.

And maybe it's time we started paying more attention to that.

Final Thoughts on Redefining Authenticity, Connection, and Activism in the Digital Age

Growing up online has been both a privilege and a challenge. I've seen the internet's power—to create movements, to connect people across the world, to shape culture in ways we never could have imagined.

But I've also seen its dangers—to our mental health, to our relationships, to our sense of self.

Now, as we move forward, we have a choice.

We can let the internet define us, or we can redefine how we engage with it.

We can choose authenticity over performance, depth over surface-level engagement, real activism over empty gestures.

We can recognize that while the internet is a part of who we are, it is *not* all that we are.

Because in the end, our lives are not meant to be perfectly curated feeds or trending hashtags.

They are meant to be lived.

Beyond the screen. Beyond the algorithm. Beyond the need for validation.

And maybe, just maybe, that's the most radical thing we can do.

Epilogue: A Letter to My Younger Self About Growing Up Online

Dear Younger Me,

I see you there, hunched over a computer screen, fingers hovering over the keyboard, carefully selecting the right words, the right photo, the right version of yourself to share with the world. I see the excitement in your eyes as you refresh the page, waiting for the likes, the comments, the digital proof that you exist, that you matter.

I wish I could tell you to close the laptop, put down the phone, and walk away. Not forever, but just long enough to remember that who you are is not something that needs to be constantly curated.

The internet will give you so much. It will make you feel seen, connected, empowered. It will introduce you to people who will shape your life in ways you can't even imagine yet. You will learn, you will grow, you will build friendships that start in comment sections and DMs but become something real.

But the internet will also take from you.

It will make you doubt yourself. It will whisper that you

are not enough—unless you edit, unless you filter, unless you perform. It will pull you into a cycle of validation and exhaustion, where your worth feels tied to engagement metrics instead of who you are when no one is watching.

You will compare yourself to people whose lives are just as carefully constructed as yours. You will think that they have it all figured out, that they are prettier, funnier, more successful. You will forget that behind every flawless post is a moment of self-doubt, of insecurity, of loneliness that looks a lot like yours.

There will be moments when the internet feels like home and moments when it feels like a battlefield. You will witness movements that change the world and conflicts that make you question humanity. You will speak out, and you will stay silent. You will be praised, and you will be afraid of saying the wrong thing.

And somewhere along the way, you will start to wonder: Who am I outside of this?

I wish I could tell you that balance is easy, that reclaiming your sense of self is as simple as unplugging. It's not. The internet will always be a part of your life. But it doesn't have to define your life.

So here's what I want you to remember:

- You are not a brand. You are not a collection of posts or a perfectly curated feed. You are a person—flawed, messy, and beautifully real.
- You don't owe the internet every part of yourself. Some moments are meant to be lived, not posted. Some thoughts are meant to be felt, not shared.
- Not every opinion deserves your energy. You don't have to argue with strangers. You don't have to prove yourself to people who don't even know you.

- Comparison is a trap. The highlight reels you scroll through are not the full story. No one has it as figured out as they seem. Not even the influencers. Not even you.
- The people who matter will be there—online or offline. The real ones won't care how often you post, how many followers you have, or whether your aesthetic is consistent. They will care about you.

One day, you will step back and realize that the internet is just a tool, not a reflection of your worth. One day, you will look in the mirror and recognize yourself again—not through the lens of a front-facing camera, not through the approval of likes, but through your own eyes.

And that, my dear younger self, will be the most freeing moment of all.

Until then, take a deep breath. Log off when you need to. Remember that who you are is enough.

Always.

With love,

Your Future Self